WOW!
Special Edition

KU-250-404

Welcome!

Hey, kids, you're in for a treat with this special edition of *WOW!* We are very lucky to have four special guest editors with us – Max, Cat, Ant and Tiger – the heroes who defeated Dr X (find out how on pages 4-7). We've got loads more awesome stuff for you to read, too.

Enjoy!

Penny Piminy

Editor in Chief

What's inside ...

1

Hero Snap Shots

Fact File: **Max**

Find out more about making your own musical instruments on pages 16-17.

Age: 9

Likes: finding things, reading, basketball, skateboarding, cycling, having adventures, making things

Dislikes: shopping, my sister waking me up early, fish fingers, evil villains

Favourite books: adventure and action books, books about how to make stuff

Favourite music: hip-hop. I like making my own instruments and making my own music, too

Favourite food: noodles

Fact File: **Cat**

Age: 9

Likes: cats (of course), cycling, computer games, reading, watching films, having adventures

Dislikes: Tiger being annoying, my sisters being annoying, anyone being annoying, flying

Favourite books: history books, funny stories, magazines. And anything by K J Sparkling but especially the Timberland Finch books

Favourite music: Pop. Stuff I can sing to – I love karaoke!

Favourite food: grated cheese sandwiches and chocolate (but not at the same time!)

Fact File: **Ant**

Age: 7

Likes: animals (any animals but especially my pet hamster, Pickles), playing on my computer, doing experiments, reading, taking photos, running, having adventures

Dislikes: baked beans, heights (falling from them), drains

Favourite books: science and nature books - books with lots of facts in. Oh, and *The Science of Running*, by Gladstone Day.

Favourite music: I'm having keyboard lessons, so I like anything I can play along to

Favourite food: spaghetti

Fact File: **Tiger**

Age: 8

Likes: playing football, skateboarding, swimming, reading comics, having muddy adventures!

Dislikes: being bored, spiders, having baths

Favourite books: books about sport, books about big trucks, comics

Favourite music: rock and pop. Anything loud with drums!

Favourite food: toast and marmalade

GREENVILLE NEWS

Scientist X Behind Bars!

Dr X, one of the most respected scientists at NICE (National Institute for the Creation of Energy), has been arrested. Following an investigation by Inspector Textor of the Greenville City Police Department, he was taken into custody yesterday for questioning.

Greenville's most up-to-date news

Monday 4th July

Shrinking Plot EXposed

It turns out that Dr X's ground-breaking work for NICE has been a cover for a more sinister operation. In his hideout underneath the NICE building, Dr X has been busy building NASTI (Nano Science and Technology Inc). NASTI has been developing a secret weapon called the X-machine. The X-machine has the power to shrink things to micro-size. Dr X intended to use his machine to shrink the world so that he could be the greatest and most powerful person in it! But unfortunately for Dr X, he was shrunk to micro-size in the process.

Thanks to the heroic exploits of four brave children, Max, Cat, Ant and Tiger, from Green Bank School, Dr X's plans have come to nothing. It is thought that the children, along with the scientist Dani Day, helped to foil Dr X's plans. Dani Day, recently promoted to Senior Scientist at NICE, managed to restore Dr X to normal size so he could be safely locked away. Although the full story has not yet been told, the children are due to be interviewed today at the famous WOW! magazine where all will be revealed.

Reply Forward

Dear Mayor,

Further to my last email, I wanted to let you know that Dr X is safely locked up in jail. We had a lucky escape there. The world was in great danger. Dr X was going to shrink everything! He shrunk the Empire State building in New York, the Sydney Opera House and the Eiffel Tower. He even wanted to shrink the Sphinx in Egypt! These kids have saved the world. They were too smart for Dr X.

Regards
Inspector Textor
Inspector, Greenville
City Police Dept.

 Reply Forward

Hi there, Inspector

Yes, I thoroughly agree. The children are real heroes. I can't imagine what it would have been like if Dr X's plan had succeeded, can you? We must think of a suitable reward for them – any ideas? ☺

Best wishes

Rita Wright
Mayor of Greenville

Things to do

Write a draft email back to the Mayor as if you are Inspector Textor.

K J Sparkling — Up Close and Personal

The well-known author K J Sparking speaks to one of our guest editors, Cat, about writing and rats!

Cat Hi K J. I'm very pleased to meet you. I've read all your Timberland Finch books.

K J Hello to you, Cat. I'm glad you like my stories.

Cat Where did you get the idea for a series of books about a boy who can turn into any animal he wants and then helps to solve crimes?

K J It's a question I get asked a lot. I'm not sure about other writers, but I don't go out looking for ideas - they come and find me! With Timberland it started with a daydream. When you get older, people try and tell you that daydreaming is not a good idea. But I think it is a fantastic way to spend your time, just sitting and staring and letting your imagination run wild. I thoroughly recommend a good daydream every day (of course, not when you're in lessons kids!). Anyway, one day, I was just sitting staring out of the window, watching a bird - a greenfinch - and I thought 'Wouldn't it be great if someone could just turn into a bird?'. And then this character just strolled into my head.

Cat So you knew everything about Timberland straight away?

K J Not quite. If only writing was as easy as daydreaming! Then the hard work began. I had to give him a shape, size, hairstyle and eye colour - all the things that make him into a real person. Then I had to think about what he likes and dislikes. As a writer, my job is to put my characters in situations that are exciting, dangerous or uncomfortable, so I have to know how they are going to react. It's like getting to know a new friend.

Things to do Why not spend 5 minutes daydreaming and then try and make up your own new character?

Cat What is your favourite animal that you like turning Timberland into?

K J It would have to be a rat. I have a pet rat, called Winston.

Cat What made you pick a rat for a pet?

K J Rats are misunderstood. They are actually intelligent, friendly creatures and hardly ever bite (unless you try to annoy them). Rats are very clean and are constantly grooming themselves to keep tidy. I wish I could keep so clean and tidy all the time! Oh, and they are also active at night. I work best at night, so Winston keeps me company.

Cat I don't like their tails.

K J They are a bit scaly, but you get used to them.

Fact File: **Winston**

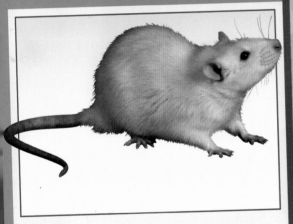

Age: 1

Likes: a nice fresh bed of hay, climbing up things, chewing bits of wood, escaping

Dislikes: being by himself, being hungry

Favourites music: he does seem to get a bit excited when there is some heavy metal on the radio

Favourite food: a slice of apple once a week (with the pips removed)

Fact File: **K J Sparkling**

Age: it's a secret!

Likes: meeting new people, reading magazines (especially *WOW!*), my pet rat, Winston

Dislikes: not finishing things, Winston escaping, losing things

Favourite books: romance and thrillers

Hobbies: daydreaming, writing, ice skating (watch out for my new TV show *Sparkling On Ice*)

Favourite music: jazz and classical

Favourite food: cornflakes with ice cold milk. Oh, and biscuits. I always have a packet of biscuits next to me when I'm working

Bot the difference!

See if you can spot the 10 things that are different in the bottom picture.

Before

After

Answers on p.40

12

The Big Green Poem Page

Eco worrier

I'm an eco worrier
I'm worried about our planet
I'm an eco worrier
How much warmer can it get?

I'm an eco worrier
I'm worried about melting ice caps
I'm an eco worrier
They're dripping off the map.

I'm an eco worrier
I'm worried about polar bears
I'm an eco worrier
Soon they'll be sitting on deckchairs.

I'm an eco worrier
I'm worried about penguins
I'm an eco worrier
They'll need sunscreen for their wings.

I'm an eco worrier
I'm worried about our planet
I'm an eco worrier
How much warmer can it get?

Nathan, aged 10

Remember to recycle
Everything you can:
Clothes, paper, tins and plastic,
Your old pots and pans -
Collect them up, put them in the right box.
Landfill sites are filling up,
It makes me cross!
No more waste – there's no more space!
Go green, recycle, and save the human race.
Amy, age 9

Did you know ...

Did you know that this type of poem is called an *acrostic* poem? The letters down the left hand side spell out a word, too.

??

Big Green Planet

It's big, it's green,
It's the best planet
I've ever seen.
Dotty, aged 6

Turn off the taps

Join in my rap,
Turn off the taps,
Let's get hip
Don't let them drip
Get in the bath –
Don't make me laugh!
I'll have a shower,
To save water and power.
Jacob, aged 7

Things to do Can you make up your own Big Green Poem? Why not try an acrostic poem using the letters in your name?

Beginners' Guide to Skateboarding

① Safety first

Skateboarding is great fun, but it is difficult. You could fall off so you must wear pads and a helmet. You also need a pair of flat bottomed shoes – they have better grip.

Skateboarding is one of my favourite things in the whole world! It's harder than it looks, but here are some tips to help you get started.

② Get to know your board

deck

front

back

trucks

wheels

Don't spend a lot of money on a board to start with. Good boards can be pretty expensive and you might find that you don't like skateboarding after all. Get advice from a good skateboarding shop.

③ Getting started

Before you try moving, you will need to get comfy standing on your board. Practise on the floor in your bedroom. First, put one foot on the back (just above the truck) and the other foot in the middle of the board. Your feet should be side on. You need to work out if you feel better with your right or left foot at the front of the board. Move your feet into different positions and see how it feels.

Warning, kids!

Make sure you take a grown-up with you when you are learning.

4 Pushing off

Take your board outside and find a smooth, level surface. Put your front foot over the front truck with your toes facing forwards. Use your back foot to push off – imagine you are walking and taking a step. Don't push too hard to start with. When the skateboard starts rolling, put your back foot on the back of the skateboard in the position you have been practising.

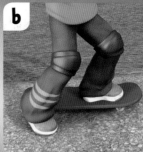

5 Turning

When you have a bit of speed, the easiest way to turn is to put a bit more weight into your heels or toes, depending on which way you want to turn. There are other ways too, but these are more tricky.

6 Stopping

There are a few different ways to stop, but the easiest way is to take your back foot off and drag it on the ground.

Another way to stop is to do a **tail stop**, or **heel break**. This is where you step down on the tail (back) of the skateboard, pushing it into the ground. The front of your board will come up into the air but your foot will still be on it.

Turning also slows you down.

It takes a lot of practice to stop safely, so you should try it when you are going very slowly to begin with.

Max Makes ...

> Do you enjoy listening to music? Well, why not try making your own instruments?

Chimes

What you will need:
- 6 tall glasses, glass bottles or jam jars
- water
- spoon
- food colouring

What you need to do ...
1. Fill your bottles or jars with different amounts of water.
2. Play your chimes by gently striking the glasses with a spoon.

You can colour your chimes by putting some food colouring in the water. Each note or glass can have a different colour.

! Warning, kids!

This instrument is safe, but broken glass can be dangerous, so don't hit your chimes too hard!

?? Did you know ...

Pitch is how low or high a sound is. The more water in the glass, the lower the pitch will be. Less water will give you a higher pitch. Wooden and metal spoons will make different sounds – try experimenting with both.

Finger drum kit

What you will need:

- 5 cardboard tubes (kitchen roll tubes or toilet roll tubes)
- some balloons
- sticky tape
- pencils or pens
- scissors

What you need to do ...

1. Cut the cardboard tubes into different lengths (you may want to get a grown-up to help)
2. Cut the small end off of five balloons.
3. Stretch each balloon over the end of each of the tubes.
4. Use some sticky tape to secure the balloons to the tubes. Then tape all of the tubes together.
5. Decorate your mini drum kit with pens or pencils.
6. Play your drums using your fingers or using two pencils!

If you want to experiment with bigger drums, try using wooden spoons as drumsticks and use upturned flower pots, tin cans or dustbin lids as drums. But don't forget to ask permission first!

Why not get together with some friends and make your own band?

Things to do

Once you have got used to your instrument, try counting out the beat: 1 and 2, 1 and 2, 1 and 2. Then try 1, 2, 3, 4, 1, 2, 3, 4. Then try making up your own beat.

17

A Day in the life of
Dani Day

WOW!

Another   Exclusive ...

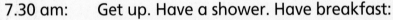

When Dr X was sent to jail, I was promoted to Senior Scientist at NICE so my day has changed quite a bit from when I had to hide in the drains ...

7.30 am: Get up. Have a shower. Have breakfast: fruit, yoghurt or porridge.

8:15 am: Cycle to work.

8:45 am: Get to work. Check my emails. Plan my day.

9:00 am: Have a team meeting.

9:30 am: Go to the lab and start work. I am currently working on a project to produce energy by using bacteria grown in old shoes. It is a natural process and completely environmentally friendly, but it is a bit smelly.

12:00 pm: Go to the staff canteen for lunch. I normally have sandwiches.

1:00 pm: This part of my day varies. Sometimes I go back to the lab. Sometimes I go out to local schools and give talks about science.

3:00 pm: Back at my desk: typing up notes, updating my lab book, reading, planning my next experiments.

4.30 pm: Prepare any experiments that I need to leave overnight.

5:15 pm: Home time!

What made you become a scientist?

My dad, Gladstone Day, was a great scientist. He was always telling me really interesting stuff when I was little. I got the bug from him!

Best parts of the job

There is a lot of variety in the job. I never know quite what I am going to find when I come in in the morning! I love exploring new ideas and I like to feel that my work is making a difference in the world.

Worst parts of the job

You need a lot of patience to do a job like this. Sometimes it can take a long time to find out why an experiment will work or not. You may have to do the same experiment many times before it goes right.

Things to do

Why not write your own 'Day in the life ...' about what you get up to?

19

Being a Henchman

Think you've got what it takes to be a henchman?

Being a henchman is not as easy as it looks. You may think it's all standing in the background and giving the occasional evil snigger but there is much more to it than that.

Socket's Top Ten Henchman Tips

1. Practise the words "Yes, Boss," and "No, Boss" a lot. A good henchman needs to do exactly what their boss says.

2. Invent a good nickname. Working for an evil genius means that you want to keep your real identity secret. My real name is … Oh, you nearly had me there!

3. Get lots of disguises. The boss may need you to go undercover.

4. Practise sitting still for a long time without falling asleep. There are times when your boss will say, "Sit there and watch that screen." So you have to sit there and watch the screen. Sometimes for hours.

5. Learn to make tea. Evil geniuses tend to take a lot of tea breaks.

6. Know your mops! The boss is always asking us to clean stuff – the worst is cleaning the NASTI toilets.

7. Don't ask questions – or not too many of them. These always seem to make the boss mad for some reason.

8. Practise standing still for a long time. This is the same as number 4, but the boss says, "Stand there and guard that!"

9. You will need a hard head. So that when the boss throws things at you, they bounce off.

10. Practise your snigger (an essential part of the job). You have to laugh at all your bosses jokes – even if they are not funny. So get your friends to tell you lots of jokes and make sure you laugh!

Animal Jokes!

Why did the rubber chicken cross the road?

To stretch its legs.

Why did the chicken cross the basketball court?

The referee called a fowl.

Why do bees hum?

Because they can't remember the words.

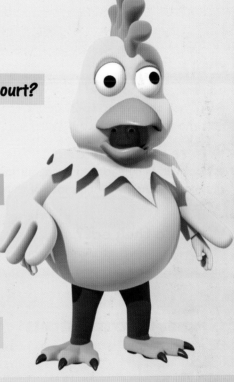

How can you find out all about spiders?

By looking at a website.

Which mouse was a famous Roman emperor?

Julius Cheeser.

Which day of the week do chickens hate most?

Fry-day.

Where do ants go for their holidays?

Frants.

Why did the chicken cross the playground?

To get to the other slide.

21

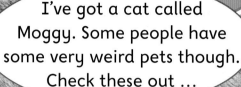

I've got a cat called Moggy. Some people have some very weird pets though. Check these out ...

Chinchillas

Chinchillas are soft and furry with big bushy tails and big ears. They can live up to 20 years. They are shy, but they can become tame enough to handle.

Where do they live?

A chinchilla will need a large cage, indoors. They love climbing, so they will need lots of things to climb on in the cage.

What do they eat?

Chinchillas are vegetarians. Specially prepared chinchilla pellet food is available and they should also have plenty of fresh hay.

Giant African Snails

Giant African land snails are fairly easy to look after. You can pick them up by their shells (with clean hands) but you must be careful because their shells can get damaged easily. They can reach up to 25 centimeters and live up to nine years.

Where do they live?

You'll need a large tank to keep them in and special heating in their tanks. The tank will need to be sprayed with water to keep it damp.

What do they eat?

Snails are very healthy – they like lots of vegetables! They also need calcium so they will need a cuttlefish bone, crushed eggshells, or crushed chalk.

Snakes

Snakes are certainly not cute! But they can be a good option for anyone allergic to fur. Corn snakes are a good choice for new snake owners as they tend to be gentle. Always get advice on what snake is best for you.

Where do they live?

A secure, escape-proof tank is essential. Special tanks, called *vivariums*, are available to buy. The snake will need somewhere to hide and climb. Different species have different needs – always ask an expert for help.

What do they eat?

Snakes are fussy eaters. They only eat when they are hungry. They will live on a diet of mice and rats (some larger snakes eat rabbits).

Tarantulas

Tarantulas may be furry, but they don't like being stroked or held. They also possess venom and can bite humans. But most bites rarely cause anything more than aching around the area.

Where do they live?

You will need a tank if you want to keep a tarantula. A small glass fishtank with a plastic lid is fine. You will need one or two small ventilation holes in the lid. Your tarantula will need somewhere to hide and special heating in their tanks, too. Tarantulas must be kept on their own – otherwise they might eat other tarantulas!

What do they eat?

Captive tarantulas eat live crickets but they will eat a wide variety of other insects. These can be bought from mail-order companies and from specialist pet shops.

GREENVILLE NEWS

X Escapes!

The famous criminal Dr X has escaped! "He was there when I locked up last night," said his guard, Joe Malone. "But when I checked this morning, he had gone! I don't know how he got out."

The mystery deepens because his mum, Mrs X, who was recently arrested for trying to steal the WOW! Award for being Wonderful, was still in the cell. She is refusing to talk about what happened. Inspector Textor has asked the people of Greenville to be on their guard. Who knows what he might do next?

WANTED!

The criminal known as Dr X

Last seen: Greenville City Jail.

Description: 4ft 5, brown hair, angry look on his face.

Crimes: shrinking famous buildings. Attempted world domination.

Other info: considered dangerous – if spotted should not be approached.

Call Inspector Textor immediately on: Greenville 332 211.

Things to do

Design your own Wanted poster!

X Escape Theories

Shrink theory: Dr X may have managed to sneak a shrinking device into the prison, so that he could shrink himself down to micro-size and escape undetected.

We have several theories on how Dr X escaped …

Accomplice theory: Dr X had help.

Postal theory: Dr X used a large box to post himself out of jail.

1st Class

To: Far away from here

Things to do

Talk or write about how you think **Dr X** escaped.

My Son is Innocent!

Mrs X claims her son is innocent. What do you think, kids?

"My son is innocent! He's a good boy, not some crazy, so called, evil genius. Those pesky children claim that he wanted to shrink the world! Ha, the very idea. It's a whopper of a lie.

The X-machine is really a growing machine. It just went wrong. My son was going to use it to make things bigger. Think about it … no one ever need go hungry again. He could increase fruit and vegetables to the size of houses! The fact that he wanted to charge a small fee for it is neither here nor there. He is innocent I tell you.

By the way, can someone get me out of here – I'm innocent too!"

X-bots Explained

X2

PRIMARY AIM: Spying

USES: Tracking
Filming and recording
Holographic playback
Computer plug-in memory device

TOOLS: Eye cameras
Sharp jaws
Memory stick in back

STRENGTHS: Being small and fast

WEAKNESSES: Magnets
Rats

NASTI RATING: X X X X X

X1

PRIMARY AIM: Recording device

USES: Tracking
Filming and recording
Holographic playback

TOOLS: Eye cameras

STRENGTHS: Being small and fast

WEAKNESSES: Being stood on
Other X-bots

NASTI RATING: X X X X X

X3

PRIMARY AIM: Retrieval of watches

USES: Tracking   Floating
Flying   Digging
Attacking

TOOLS: Eye cameras   Foot floats
Sharp jaws   Nose drill
Helicopter blades

STRENGTHS: Being aggressive

WEAKNESSES: Magnets   Pit traps
Water balloons   Ducks

NASTI RATING: X X X X X

X-POD

PRIMARY AIM: Transport of 1 or 2 X-bots

USES: Transport

TOOLS: Helicopter blades
Retractable legs
5 gear function
3 speed function

STRENGTHS: Being very fast

WEAKNESSES: Being driven badly
Crashing

NASTI RATING: X X X X X

NANO-BOT

PRIMARY AIM: Micro-spying

USES: Tracking
Filming and recording
Computer plug-in memory device

TOOLS: Eye cameras   Zoom lenses
Filming and recording
Memory stick in back

STRENGTHS: Being very small so they can
go unseen

WEAKNESSES: Being stood on
Being lost

NASTI RATING: X X X X X

X-CRAFT

PRIMARY AIM: Transport a squad of X-bots

USES: Transport
Capture

TOOLS: Helicopter blades
Retractable legs   Hyper-speed
Retractor/shrinking beam
8 gear function
6 speed function

STRENGTHS: Being very fast

WEAKNESSES: Being driven badly
Crashing

NASTI RATING: X X X X X

Cat and Tiger's book review

These are our favourite books. What are yours?

Horrible Histories – The Vile Victorians
Author: Terry Deary

Plot: This book tells you everything horrible that you want to know about the Victorians – how they lived, what they wore and what sports they played. It is very funny and has lots of interesting facts.

Excitement: 3/10   Fear factor: 1/10   Easy read: 7/10   Humour: 9/10

War Horse
Author: Michael Morpurgo

Plot: This is about a horse called Joey who gets sent off to France during the First World War. His owner, a boy called Albert, joins up as a soldier and tries to find him. It is told from Joey's point of view and tells you what it was like for horses that were used in battles. It is a sad story but it has a happy ending.

Excitement: 9/10   Fear factor: 10/10   Easy read: 5/10   Humour: 1/10

The Adventures of Captain Underpants
Author: Dav Pilkey

Plot: Two boys, George and Harold, create their own comic book superhero called Captain Underpants. Things get tricky when they hypnotize their principal, Mr Krupp, who starts to believe he really is Captain Underpants and tries to take on some baddies!

Excitement: 8/10   Fear factor: 3/10   Easy read: 9/10   Humour: 10/10

Secret Agent Jack Stalwart – The Search for the Sunken Treasure: Australia
Author: Elizabeth Singer Hunt

Plot: Jack Stalwart, the nine-year-old secret agent, has a new mission. He has to find a missing diver. But he has sharks, Komodo dragons and a dangerous pirate boss to fight! This is a really exciting adventure with cool gadgets and sunken treasure.

Excitement: 10/10   Fear factor: 7/10   Easy read: 7/10   Humour: 2/10

Charlie Small – Gorilla City
Author: Charlie Small

Plot: Charlie Small is at least four hundred years old – although he still looks the same as he did when he was eight! He is stuck in time and is very, very lost. In this exciting adventure story, he goes exploring and meets a mechanical rhino and becomes King of the gorillas.

Excitement: 9/10   Fear factor: 8/10   Easy read: 7/10   Humour: 4/10

> Why not write your own book review?

Cows in Action – The Ter-Moo-Nators
Author: Steve Cole

Plot: I didn't think cows were smart, but this book is about three clever cows (Professor McMoo, Bo and Pat) who are smarter than people. The professor builds a time machine to get away from the angry farmer's wife. They travel in time, meet Henry VIII, fight evil bulls from the future and save history!

Excitement: 8/10   Fear factor: 5/10   Easy read: 7/10   Humour: 8/10

On your marks, get set ... cook

Plug's Amazing Oven-Baked Macaroni Cheese

Ingredients:
300g short-cut macaroni
25g butter
25g plain flour
1 tsp English mustard
600ml milk
200g grated mature cheddar, or more to taste
salt and freshly ground black pepper

Equipment:
1 x large pan
1 x small pan
1 x colander
1 x wooden spoon
1 x heatproof dish

What you have to do ...
1. Preheat your oven to 375 degrees Fahrenheit/190 degrees Celsius/Gas Mark 5.
2. Cook the pasta according to the instructions on the side of the packet. Use the colander to drain thoroughly.
3. Meanwhile, you have to make a cheese sauce. Melt the butter in a pan. Slowly stir in the flour and mustard until you make a paste. Then, slowly add the milk to give a thin smooth sauce – stir continuously. Simmer for 5 minutes, stirring occasionally, then stir in the cheese until it is all melted.
4. Mix in the cooked pasta. Then transfer the mix to a heatproof dish and top with extra grated cheese.
5. Bake in the oven for approximately 20-25 mins.

Alternatives: For extra crunch you could put some plain, crushed potato crisps or crumbled wheat biscuits (extra yum!) on the top. To flavour the insides, you could add some peas or chopped leeks.

● Safety first...
Remember to get a grown-up to help you!

Socket's Secret Summer Smoothie

Ingredients:
1 x banana
5 x large strawberries
Small handful of blueberries
150ml/ ¼ pint of milk
150ml/ ¼ pint of natural yoghurt

Ingredients:
1 x large plastic jug
1 x hand blender
1 x drinking glass

What you have to do ...
1. Peel the banana and put it in the jug. Throw the waste in your compost bin.
2. Wash the strawberries and remove any stalks or greenery.
3. Wash the blueberries and add to the jug.
4. Blend the fruit together – ask a grown-up to help if you need to.
5. Slowly add the milk and the yoghurt.
6. Pour into a glass and drink!

Ant Experiments
Electromagnets

Electromagnets are magnets that run on electricity.

Making a magnet
What you will need:
- A small battery
- A nail
- Lots of thin, copper wire coated in plastic
- Some paperclips
- Sticky tape

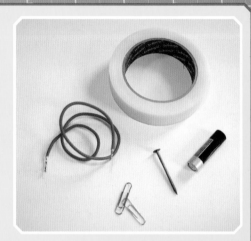

What you have to do ...

1.

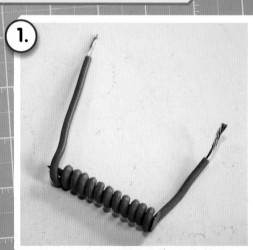

Wrap the copper wire tightly round the nail, from the flat head end to the point. The more coils you have, the stronger your magnet will be. The ends of the wire should be bare – ask a grown-up to help you if necessary.

2.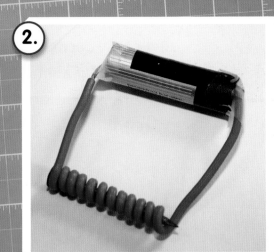

Using sticky tape, attach one end of the wire to the positive (+) end of the battery, and the other to the negative (-) end of the battery. It does not matter which wire you attach to which end.

3.

Warning, kids!

This experiment is safe, but as electricity passes through a wire, some energy is lost as heat. The battery can get hot.

You now have your electromagnet! Test it out on some metal objects like paperclips.

Find out more

For more about electromagnets see www.howstuffworks.com

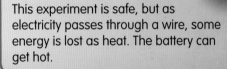

When electromagnets are not connected to electricity, they stop working. The strength of an electromagnet can be changed by changing the amount of electric current that flows through it. Electromagnets are used in many kinds of devices: electric bells, switches, door locks, and motors. The first electromagnet was invented by the British electrician William Sturgeon, in 1825.

X Marks the Spot

There have been several recorded sightings of Dr X since his escape. Have you seen Dr X?

Can you name these famous tourist spots across the world or the countries that they are in? Talk about them with your friends and share what you know. Try drawing a picture of one.

Inside NASTI

With the NASTI operation shut down, the board of directors at NICE have decided to open it up as a museum to the public. Luckily, there are two experts ready to show you around.

The X-machine: was used for shrinking and growing things. Energy was generated from 5 small devices that sat in a gold box. This was then magnified in heart of the machine and power was funneled through a small reactor pipe and up into a giant magnifying chamber. At least, that's the theory.

Welcome to the NASTI museum!

Things to do
Design your own hideout — draw and label a picture of it.

Dr X's chair: many an evil scheme was planned from his Dead Comfy 009 chair. The Dead Comfy range is surprisingly popular with evil geniuses.

Agony Ant

Ant answers some of our readers' questions.

Dear Ant
I am doing a project about ants. Where should I look up some information?
Ash (aged 7)

Dear Ant
It's my mum's birthday next week and I don't know what to get her. What should I get her?
Zarina (aged 8)

Ant's Answer: You could go to the library and try and find a book on ants to help. Or you could go on to the Internet and go to a search engine like Google, and type in the word 'ants'. It comes up with 13,800,000 different websites to look at, so you are bound to find something interesting! The kids' section of the National Geographic website is very good for finding out about the natural world.
www.nationalgeographic.com

Ant's Answer: This is quite a tricky question. Sometimes I ask my dad or my aunty and they come up with some good ideas. The presents that my mum likes best are the ones I make for her myself. You could try making her a birthday card. That would be a good start.

Ant's Answer: Maybe your little brother just wants someone to play with. Why don't you try playing with your toys together, but make a deal with him first that he is not allowed to take your toys without asking. Can you ask your mum or dad for a lock for your toy box? Otherwise, you'll need to find some good hiding places!

Dear Ant,
My little brother keeps coming into my room when I'm not there and taking my toys. Sometimes he breaks them. How can I stop him?
Paul (aged 9)

Cat's Quiz

Dr X wanted to take over the world. See if you can do any better with world domination ...

How many new words can you make from the letters in the words World Domination?

Example:
1. load
2. mint
3. rant

Come on, you can do better than that!

Answers to Bot the difference! (p.12)
1. Tiger's sleeve stripes removed
2. Blue balloon changed to red
3. Elastic band on catapult removed
4. Spoon on catapult removed
5. X-bots in sky removed
6. Wheel changed from blue to pink
7. Metal arches in background removed
8. X-bot's eyes turned blue
9. Balloon in sky removed
10. Ballon on ground removed.